Ever Truly Yours

'Reflections on Love'

Poems by
Kate Barnwell

Grosvenor Artist Management

First published in 2014 by
Grosvenor Artist Management
32/32 Grosvenor Street
Mayfair
London
W1K 4QS
www.grosvenorartistmangement.com

A CIP catalogue record for this book is available from the British Library

Front cover from an original watercolour by Evelyn Dunphy, *'Morning Glory'*
www.evelyndunphy.com

ISBN 978-0-9574980-4-4

Also available in Limited Edition hardback from www.grosvenorartistmanagement.com
with a FREE CD of readings by Tobias Menzies & Victoria Hamilton

Praise for Kate's first book *'A Collection of Poems & Lyrics'*
ISBN: 978-0-9574980-0-6

"A remarkable achievement for the young author. Her words and poems are startlingly raw and authentic. She has drawn from a deep personal reservoir that provides us with a real emotional gem."

Ivor Davis

Former Columnist, New York Times Syndicate

Former Foreign Correspondent, The Times of London and London Daily Express

"I am on my third reading and they just get better and better. I find something new each time."

Evelyn Dunphy

Award-winning watercolourist, USA

"Confident and self-assured, both traditional and modern, there is something for everyone. It has made me rediscover the pleasures of poetry."

David Chilton

Urban Fox Media, London

"I hadn't come across Kate Barnwell before...she's the real thing!
I thought the poems were outstanding!
She is one of the few poets today who can use rhyme and formal structure without it seeming remotely forced or constraining."

Peter Murray

Pharmaceuticals and Entrepreneur, UK

"Kate is clearly an incredibly talented young poet with insights beyond her age...
I think of a young Sylvia Plath or in part Elizabeth Barrett Browning.
She has a strong sense of the visual and is well on her way to integrating that successfully in her writing, for what is poetry but the handmaiden of the mind's eye."

Michael Downend

Playwright, USA

"A sometimes funny, often fragile yet haunting collection that will stay with the reader long after the last page has turned"

Rosemary Forgan

Television Producer

Foreword by the Author

Poetry offers respite in a busy and often emotionally inarticulate world.
Spanning different eras and crossing a wide and varied audience, its presence in your life and your soul is immeasurable.
Sometimes only poetry has the words to evoke images and create pictures; memories indelibly printed on the mind.
Romantic poetry provides the perfect complement to moments of love and happiness or comforting words to lean on in times of loss or despair.
The significance of poetry is as relevant to us today as ever.

Introduction

Something very wonderful is happening.

We live in a world of heightened communication with endless means of correspondence on a 24 hour basis. Technology has advanced us to the stage where we send messages to people in the same room as ourselves (as well as to those miles away). We have to justify every minute of every day.

Yet having everything at our fingertips means we are missing out, and even forgetting, how important it is to express what we feel in the spoken word and the handwritten word. We have such a richness of language to draw upon yet it is so often reduced to a meaningless text.

As with art of the past every age is given a title; the Medieval age; the Early Renaissance; the High Renaissance and Mannerism: each phase either an advancement on the other or a reaction against it.

So, something very wonderful is happening.

I want poetry to undergo its own renaissance: a revival of idealism; an emphasis on feeling; the free expression of individuality and of passions.

It's time we learnt to love again, to embroider and decorate love and to allow ourselves more time. Poetry has hidden depths and different ways of presenting thoughts. It is not surprising we look to the established poetry of Keats, Shelley, Byron, Rossetti and Browning and of course the world's most recognised writer of quotable lines of love – Shakespeare. These are authors who wrote in a style of their time, who

spoke of their feelings and imaginings and have left a profound legacy. These are the same emotions we feel today, but rarely encounter, where modern life is a business.

Poetry endures because writers capture a moment in time, preserving fleeting glimpses of life and thereby defying death. A poet's words bestow a form of immortality and with romantic poetry, by addressing a lover, ensure that lover forever holds an immortal status. This is the extraordinary power of poetry. Each reader of those words of love can claim ownership of the emotions, believing the poem to be their own. There are many risks involved both in creating and reading romantic poetry: one opens one's soul to exposure and possible ridicule – how brave are any of us?

Surely we all seek happiness in love; a caring relationship in which to develop and a soul mate to see us through life.

Kate Barnwell, 2014

Contents

Poems

Lyrics

I

POEMS

Keats: on visiting, on leaving, in memoriam
An introduction

Standing in the high-ceilinged, small corner bedroom of the first floor of the Keats-Shelley House in Piazza di Spagna, Rome, where John Keats died, is a very moving and humbling experience. The windows now look down on to 21st century life although a church bell, horses' hooves and the cries of people would have been the sounds he heard as he lay dying in 1821. There is a definite atmosphere in these few rooms where Keats lived out his last winter months.

After spending time absorbing this museum with its stories, letters and books, I walked through Rome to the Non-Catholic Cemetery to find Keats' final resting place: a sunny, violet covered, unnamed grave next to his friend Joseph Severn.

'This grave contains all that was mortal of a Young English Poet who desired these Words to be engraved on his Tomb Stone

Here lies One Whose Name was writ in Water'

It was here, at first sight, in April 1877, Oscar Wilde lay prostrate on the lawn, later writing a sonnet to commemorate the occasion of his visit - calling it 'the Holiest place in Rome'.

Keats beauty, tenderness and suffering make his poetry and memory an everlasting fascination. Acknowledged today as one of England's finest poets, his work, his words and his story continue to live on; touching and inspiring a new generation.

Keats: on visiting, on leaving, in memoriam

On pillowed head stir elliptical lashes, oh what
Peaceful fantasies catch your tempered mind
Fluttering to the rhythm of dreams, deep
In dead man's sleep, wait to lift those heavy lids
At the devoted, holy gates of Heaven
Take the keys, unlock the door and ascend
For on Earth the visible truth unfolds:
You have lived too long under sorrow's breath
While silver words whisper around your lips
Death will appear, and leave the rest of us, dismissed

Oh rally once more, show me your glassy eyes
The watery white dots like the bold, bright
Bulge of the moon; come again those smiles!
Drawn in curves across the cheeks
Dimples in playful expression, tan and line your face
Authored by the sweats and joys of life

How you could pry the secrets from the souls of men!
Convert sins to sacrifices, turn giants to gentlemen
What restive thoughts turn upon your brow and breast?
With which we sit unacquainted
They lie forever, as low as mists and unsolved mysteries.

Beyond the shuttered window panes
The bells chime in their frequent patterns
Breaking the hour quarter by quarter
Spinning the world through the day
Precious minutes where you persist,
Before the past takes hold of you:
Death takes a final stroke, and stings
Making your existence a mere concept of another age
As uncontrollable time spirals into an empty nothingness
The living sombrely recoil to recover themselves.
O, the aches and pulses pounding in my chest, my heart
Why could it not pump for us both?
And claim another victim for its rest

You made a wish one dismal dawn
For violets and daisies, like gothic cloth
To grow in splendid beauty around your memorial feet
What indescribable frankness of irony is this?
To be loved by perfect few in one life, by thousands in another
By romancing the world with fiery, impassioned leaps of
Faith in nature's greatness, watered the dryness in tongues
Fed and swelled the sleepy souls with brave ambitions
For seeing not a literal life but the magical beauty encasing it
Living long beyond the chill of graves, fluent words
Speak from page, to spread in ever-advancing worlds.

In Fields

Pass me a ribboned rosebud from its bed
And lazily lie each velvet petal
To relish as a crown around her head.
Let pollen's feverish senses settle.
Upon her crimson cheeks and fingertips
Rustles the dizzy hay and buttery corn;
In brushing her face, they may taste her lips
I'm caught by the sun's hazy hour; reborn.

Little stirs but time's distant cuckoo cry
So silence speaks, the more intense the scene
As flowers gave their bodies, so shall I
And live and breathe entirely for love's dream.
Through the green cuts of grass, fringed in sky blue
Valleys and beetles heard how I loved you.

By the Lakeside

She left me by the lakeside
It was gone noon before I knew
So that I might drown my sorrows
But my sorrows only grew

She left me as the last leaves dried
I watched them fall upon the lake
Drift out into the middle pond
Slow to catch the dying wake

She left me when I was young
Although my head had chosen well
Repeated passions keenly felt
Warming deep in heart to dwell

She left me on a Sunday
A day we shared 'til then
Each week the evil hour relived
And now I can bear no friend

She left me with no reasons why
In the pool my doomed reflection
The last light, weary, lingered on
My weight of sad complexion

In summer, the sun will surely scorch
In winter, be weak and watery.
What use are these painterly skies?
Without those sweet romantic eyes
Which I may softly muse upon
Then chase her thoughts that follow on.

Oh disappointed love!
What did I do to you,
To deserve such pain as this?
Maybe… I did love too much.
With all this world so great and wide
I sit alone… by our lakeside.

Wanderings

I hear the world in a sea-shell lip
And your voice in the wash of a wave
I sit on a rock made of ages turned
Before mute sands, not yet made

I see in the fields, the heavens born
And your face in the brightest of flowers
I feel colours bursting to scents
Time lingers in harmonious hours

I witness the rain sweeping your cheeks
Watch it mingle with salt in your eyes
Let lowly winds wipe away whispers
To dissolve and distract our goodbyes

I sense the restless need for calm
To pace upon my brow
And consume these wistful wanderings
For it is all I can allow.

Burning Shelley

When they burn him on the beach
His years too few and reckless spent;
The sentence of a largesse youth
Where indulgence took substantial toll
Lying on the sublime borders of sanity
Hinting at sharp sparks of madness
Existing on extremes
Frantically waving at oblivion.

In this dominion of dust and tides
He sold his soul to invited sin
Each pleasure filtering into sands 'til
The Godly clock raised its vengeful hand
And wiped him from all future plots.
Wild days played, those unpaid parades of stolen hearts
Take flight in smoke from smouldering ashes.

An Early Journey through Scotland

One journey, often taken but so seldom viewed
As I describe it now in this momentary state
Somehow blurred between
The early, peaky ascent of growing light
The sun young, not yet the flower of her age
And the sombre state of queasy, impatient night
The moon, waning in its deliverance
Thus day and night, one to rise and one to fade
Into the great gulf of separation that divides the daily world
Find chance equilibrium in the unattached sky
Each balancing their powers of composure onto the Earth.

It is at this point I find myself admiring
The landscape like a painter who jovially dances
With brush in stirring fancy at something
Unexpectedly hypnotic and sensational, taking
His footsteps of airy, unscathed fall
In making sight of this worldly halo of repose.

Young, fresh blues and yellows of the land
Colours, I wish to include
Palatable to the eye, but not yet named.
The scene lies serene as if never before approached
By prying, inquisitive early awakenings.

So I make a journey across simple roads
View the contours of hillsides, mellowing with drowsy clouds
In a heavenly pearliness of lines
The tranquil, steady beauty of pioneering plains
The oaks and beech woods shine in a myriad of greens
And shades of light magnify their radiance
The forest firs remain densely impenetrable.

The sounds, what of them, and their background influence
The bumps and curls of a moon-pulled river passage
Throwing, thrusting its cumbersome weight over granite rocks
In ruffian-style procedure,
Low-lying branches scratch the effervescent waters
Creasing their black-ironed spine
Until gradually the flow bends,
Curving into gentle pools of shallow softness
Passively preserving its precious source of purity
Blink and the years flash back
Little change, still the same continuous motion.

A stag, purveyor of his morn, stands undisturbed
His long, deep rooted heritage secure
The dew dipped grasses at dawn
The ferns and tufts about his feet
Aware, but unperturbed at my passing

No move in his establishment, no fear prickles his coat
As we both share in the sweet and honeyed tones;
The chatty, busy utterances of birds, no one alone
But a chorus of mellifluous song
Tunes overfill my ear with such intensity.
One by one the distant, solid, dark brown cows
Raise their heads and puff their warm
Steamy breaths of air: in, out and up
Onto a furrowed brow.

Soon southern blues push their northern nightly foes
Further up; their dark-bred cousins dissipate
A new daytime settles in the sky
A longer-lasting, more familiar form
How rapid, how descriptive were those ever-dying minutes
Of early morning, of late retreating night
How I might recall them when I reach my final destination
All etched and sketched within a memory bank
Their mysteries and solitude, their simplicities and details
All condensed by paints and pens till oils and inks run dry
What I have seen, lived, breathed and tasted too
One tiny temperate clime, on a tilted globe of seas.

Good Day

How to begin? Well, with good in good day!
Sipping in the newness of the morning.
A drunken, happy bee, sweet on honeys made
Should he gaze wantonly on you, like me.
Every flower blooms brighter, rhythms grow
Inside my soul, on breeze, some outreaching part
Plays love's appealing tune in youthful flow.
Felt on pulses inclining to the heart.
There is something of you in everything.
If some, one person spoke, I daresay I heard
Not one sound, nor held one listening ear.
The dulling of day will not dampen: I sing
Oh overwhelming world, full of fascinations
Not *one* can interest me now, not as she can!

The Sticks of Life

The sticks of life, on purpose strike
To break these bones to make me fall
I find a tree to help me rise
And in its branches birds can call

The stones of life make marks and scars
To hurt us each with forceful wrath
I find a rock to help me up
Whose beauty cracks, but is not lost

When angry words hang in the air
Their desperate need to burn my heart
To pierce and damage all they must
Till kindness waters well its part

I passed beyond this dark and gloom
From emptiness to energy
To proclaim the unexpected
That my wish was granted me

So, to all the sticks of life
In vain disguises you may come
I keep my spirit strong and free
Which I have made and it makes me.

Sleep

We parted once in shallow dreams
In wakefulness you'd gone
Where you had come and whence you went
Sat lost to last night's song

Daylight stings, burning into dreams
Infrequent, they appear
Deep in a sleepy mountain, vast
And past the pool of tears

Conceived upon a pillowcase
See two contented hearts
And sympathetic minds exist
Concealed within the dark.

Hearts

We talk of hearts, we draw them red
Plump and rosy and swollen shaped
Their equal contours defined and spread
And side by side our names are draped

I see skin of porcelain beauty
Gentle to touch; pure perfection
Like the dewy, drooping snowdrop
Dripping in wet pearls of reflection

The sweet silver-coated almond heart
This soft symbol of sleepy dreams
Its chocolate-covered, scented centre
Beating bright sparks of sunray beams

A picture to fix all hopes upon
Sketched on pages, admired by pen
Turn a leaf and each heart lives on
And there I write our names again.

Golden Throne

If I made you out of soft sandstone
Mould you fine
And bring you home
To sit beside me
On a golden throne
A smile for a laugh
A line for a lie
The face can turn
But cannot hide
To sit beside me
As years fall by
On a golden throne
You and I.

Now all I see is icy stone
Vain and bitter
            Callous bones
The masquerade is all your own
Your credits, your praises
         Your great self-esteem
Jewels of pride in a fantasists' scheme

Life chips away
            Crumbling with sighs
A thin veneer exposed
         To my sad, tricked eyes
I grieve, at the damage of deception.

I sat beside you, and watched you die
On pitted throne,
                        reigned in acid lies.

I Let the Devil into the House

I let the devil into the house
I did not know he came about
He disguised himself in some fine frame
His careful aim, his polite refrain

First he seemed pleasant enough
Soon reeled me in with cunning bluff
His calm composure; no cause for alarm
A warm accent, a sincere charm

Slowly the spell grew tired and thin
The darker man revealed within
His venom spat out nasty words
Bruising, scornful taunts, were heard

He convinced me of lie upon lies
He played and liked to fantasise
His tasteless, cynical, sharp remarks
Shot to a saddened, hurting heart

Who can tell the devil, in a crowd of kindly faces?
He leaves senses shattered, securities misplaced
Who will know when he, anew, will choose to come again?
The danger of a devil;
                              the deceitful, cheating friend

Look out; lock out, for
You may be young and innocent
Your judgement may be poor
Without a wakeful warning
You let the devil through the door.

A Piazza

In brushed piazzas the palm lines of city spirit
Lie revealed in the textured, scratchy cobbled stones
Of burnt umber; preserved and pickled into place
They provide the solid steps on which all life gathers
Every sentient person dispersing
Performing a daily theatre of duties

Flanked on either side stand long, parallel passages
Of curved colonnades; their symmetrical spine columns
In a mellow, dusky pink.
The cracked walls of yellow ochre sink into the outlines
And smoky dusts are wrapped into crevices

From a half-shuttered window, invisible notes
Are released from their strings
They climb onto a breeze, spin tirelessly in currents
Rise steadily, pulling at chords
Then disappear like musical balloons
Up into an atmosphere of wild abandonment
Carrying with them the bars of a fore-telling tune

Listening above in an intensity of frenzy
The rounded cherubs and putti dance in heightened relief
To the extreme corners of their frieze
Plastered into an ever-exhausted state of joy
Flaunting their giddy flesh, their uncontrollable dizziness
To a backdrop of abundant, lively swags of fruit.
The last light stretches its warming hand
Catching the tiny, tesserae of polished glass
Pinched into a holy pediment of elaborate pictures

In the final act, as an unconcerned sun sets to the west,
Vanishing to its point of perspective
A playful God takes flippantly to skimming clouds,
Neat and flat like saucer coins, across the skies
Where they dissolve into an inky bowl of blue
And a zealous dark descends to inaudible applause
Leaving the square blind to view.

Four Days with You

In those four days with you
I lived a year
No details, no consequence
I regained my real self
And in doing so took back my life.

What you gave me was love and meaning
Steeped in sensitivity and strength
Qualities re-founded, unearthed

How I wanted to leave,
To just go, to join you
Without regret or shame.
I could turn out the light,
Walk out the door
For I know I have never loved anyone, more

Yet I could not turn my back
On those I had created,
Who needed me.

You helped me to survive this path
I thank you for that.
For us, tomorrow will always be
Where life takes you away

In body and in soul
I have been adored.
I keep close every single thought
Of those days we spent together
Each one, two, three and four.

It's not the fear of the destination
But the impossibility of the journey.

In What Way can I come to You?

If I am caged by walls of brick
My windows paned in smoky glass
Thick lines of steel to bar a view
In what way can I come to you?

If my doors are chained and locked
Watched by a spying camera lens
These heavy, dark, restricted rooms
In what way can I come to you?

If I spend my days in isolation
Wasted hours roll on to weeks
My arms, my legs cry out for use
In what way might I come to you?

There is a world inside my mind
Where nature kindly hosts me
A fair, imparted transient prayer
Unites us in eternity

It lasts as long as I can hold it
Held deep beneath my mental edge
Before I'm drowned in truth unending
Left to fight this earthly dread

This is the way I come to you
I find you living in my head
Here love is made and promised
Where my captured heart is led.

Too Soon

I thought he might propose to me
Amid early buds in bloom
With outstretched arms like willow's tree
But it was all too, all too soon

Gusts force fresh flowers to the ground
Confetti winds falsely loom
Delicate shapes crushed and browned
For it was all too, all too soon

Savoured drops of oak-barrelled wine
No-longer toast a pleasant hour
Fine measures of another time
Once raised; sit shunned and soured

Two cruelly whispered, simple words
Pound on inner ear's defence
Wrap wounds to separate our worlds
In abandoned decadence

But self-respect returns its charms
And my mortal pool of thoughts
From painful breast of shadowed harms
Comes a strong, objective course

No more misguiding eye can frame me
I am undiscovered sight
Uncontrolled, no flame dare claim me
I make the turn; take full flight.

Agatha Mae

She placed a crown on curls of grey
Brushed the tentacles of outcast hair
Surveyed her dressing table of tools
And diligently manufactured her stare

Puffed pale and downy skin with powder
Let atoms of crimson blush the creases
Lifting the lost and shadowed features
Smoothing the crowded lines to please her

She lengthened her lashes to widen her eyes
Plumped her lips with the kiss of a stick
Painted each cheekbone to gleam in the light
Defined the mouth, once more, with a lick

In March she received not a bunch of mimosa
No bright smudge of yellow to lighten her eye
The gold planets of pollen, once chosen for her
A stem of blossoming suns of the sky

After an hour was hung she wept for her youth
All too fleeting its passing had been
Even devoted birds, plumed into symmetry
Abandoned their beds for new dreams

For vanity she grooms, cast by a new age
Combing her pride and her soul back in place
Reluctant to feel an ounce disengaged
Stands determined to live life apace.

Sonnet 14

The man I love, he maybe called a Prince
For every time I close my vivid eyes
There is no other sense of vision since
Who presses on the curling grip of smiles
Unaltered and as real as Spring is true
His every symbol: by Heaven confessed
Romanced and paraded in purest blue
Breathing in moods of sweet-found dreams, no less

So trim the fringes of a tempered flair
Renounce forever future fears of loss
Never judge yourself, by yourself compared
Gaze on eternal scoops of happiness
Fair and fine, unwavering steadiness
In loving, you give life, as life expects.

A Sleepless Night

No shroud of influencing dark can shake
The ceaseless, seeking conscience of my mind
And woeful frets worsen while awake
With nightly foes and teeming fears, they bind

I lie still, shadow-less and un-empowered
A stream of flipping anguishes and frights
Force me to pass each cosy clock hour
Trapped with the inertia of the night

What sophistry to leave wishes on stars
Those distant sparkling bulbs in soundless skies
Whose glint in darkness blinks to all afar
They no more answer to my plaintive cries

How the dark does exaggerate a dread
Impeaches all my sensibilities
Such deep, intangible thoughts lie abed
So farewell to peace-felt tranquilities

O melt tedious black, fall to coloured rise!
Of sunny optimism; brighter beams
Allow this staining rage to subside
Resume the natural need of reveries

Shield me from extravagant inventions
Break the mask of the pre-dawn light
Give me a pattern of sweet affections
Hurry me safely through the night.

One Look at your Face

One look at your face
Shows a silent complaint
So once full of chase
Now an hour purpose late.
The dark was our cover
To shelter our hearts
And love one another
Till the dawn raised arc

The cold just one reason
To hug and to hold
Through flourishing season
Embraced in your fold.
Warmth made of passion, to
The light of your name
Beyond a first fashion
Burn long, favoured flames

Must I think of this still?
As you call on its end
Bringing over death's chill
And the cull of dear friends.
I grieve at lost kisses
As your soul floats elsewhere
In truth, faith is missing
Only bursts of despair

How the shine of soft silk
Lies thin on fine brilliance
The rose petal shall wilt
In its loss of resilience.
My tears fall for sadness
Weeping on for our joy
Wounds of man's elusiveness
Charms made of boy

In years from now
When plunged into fate
When the talents of love
Fight the talons of hate
And we meet while in passing
At some intimate place
How will my heart sting!
At the turn of your face.

Left to Cry

A yellow canary sings falling chords
In some dark forgotten corner
He calls to his lost master
For a bowl of cooling water

See a baby in cotton-white bed
Sobbing for his missing mother
Who finds herself entwined and lost
With her elusive lover

A moaning cat, shut out at night
His mews cushioned between dark barks
House coldly closed, forced to stray
Pushed to paw a waif-like way

Dear desperate girl, in the graveyard
Her heavy tears fall plump on cheeks
Spilt for an incurable loss
Her impatient sense of grief

A weighty sound of impossible pain
Obey its mournful course
For little comfort can be gained
From lonely cries of force.

Are those your true eyes?

Are those your true eyes?
Caught wildly in first flush of April's dance
With every blink, they hug the contours
Of my soft, unchanging face
And carefully, repeating my name
Compose a daring fool's advance

Will those eyes act out the workings of your soul?
Curve rainbows; fill their stores with pots of gold
Will your inner voice reveal a lust for passions goal?
When offered hands are, 'not all you wish to hold'

How many reasons must our two hearts give?
I feel it too; we long to leap
Beyond the borders of this friendship
To love the ways of courting; for it may be
As perfect as white bunched blossoms to tree
Untainted by the pigment of any coloured siege

This season's day asks to be preserved
Remembered in growing, detailed glory.
Your vision is all for me and all be mine
In the charm of roses; fragrant beauties bind.

Across

Across the clouds appears a pink-ploughed sky
On Earth we drift, to Heaven we fly
First grounded by roots, then lifted by winds
Paths of a journey, songs sung of Kings
Take heed of the sea, inherit the land
The power of soul, working on man
His worth in the world blurs Godly defeat
Etched into time by sacred life's sleep.

Train

Go then and be gone!
Leave me please, for now as one
Take the train and make no slight glance
No shy stirring of the head, or sudden eye
Or twist of manly contours, stirred
No angled raise of shaking hand, blurs goodbye
To me, where I linger, on this ever-fixed spot.
But before you go, I never loved you more, or
Self-confessed a thousand lovely thoughts
Then wished I might forever rest
My face upon yourself
A curl of hair, a soft, protective arm
A white, caressing shirt
Your forgiving turn of cheek, silently warmed
A little while since, in a cherry load of kisses
Your ready outline, charcoal traced, on the solid platform.
The further away I watched you walk
In this crowded, grey painting
I never loved or looked for you more.
In your palette of lapis blue.

Go then and be gone!
Leave if you must, depart at the minute
No more intimate hour
Like the one which passed before
No seconds ever ticked.
The tall hand simply crept
And chimed the hour at Time's request.
Only your outbound steps, sound a heavy thud
And beat within my heart, as unifying love.
Until the golden sun has covered the moon
Until the stars have sparkled their last rays
Of flashy, silver strife
Double creaming lovers' wishes
Who lock hopes upon the night
Until the starlings have circled, settled all life
The sparrows have dusted, then flown
For now, go and be gone!
Until your train pulls home
Whistling 'I never loved you more.'
I wait patient upon the clock.

My Love for You

My love for you is spelt in stars
Is weaved by threads in tapestries.
On fruits the dimples of their flesh
Show prints upon their dewy skins
To declare in blushing comfort
What my heart so gladly brings.
As clouds know of a deeper blue
Skies cradle birds to swell the view

My love for you burns candle-bright
Is shown by everlasting flowers,
They stretch from field to weathered beach
To sway in never-ending hours.
And milky, silk shells tell the time
Of aging seas; their worldly powers
As oceans call on other shores
My love's perfection strengthens more

Washed by rivers that pass through trees
As pure as each new century.
For you, love lies beyond the pen,
Surpassed by an impassioned verse
Let me pause these fleeting days
To keep our presence undisturbed.
Come life, come love and so be true
Eternal is my love for you.

If I grow old

There's a cottage by the sea
Where I wish to grow old
Along a seaweed grass lane
Push a gate of driftwood, see
Pearly shells scatter the porch
A view of weathered cliffs
Where fish eagles take flight
On current captured breezes
Diving and spinning white flecks
Of downy under-breast
Catch a watery-silver reflection

From the cottage by the sea
Where I wish to grow old
A magnificent expanse of deep
Blue, green, ultramarine; channels
Travelled by specks of sailing ships
Over the orb, charting their course
Following the tidal laws; vessels
Flying a flag of indefatigable hope
On the horizon surface; full hearts
In the knowledge of home

At dawn the planets retreat, weakened
Paled by the prospect of waking to the bright
Beams of the sun as she resurrects herself
Into a glorious beginning

Two smiling faces follow the warmth
Like sunflower heads on the mossy lawn
Two comfortable chairs beside ruffled blanket
Pollen fairies freshly released from folds.
At the cottage by the sea
It's where I wish us to be
If I grow old.

Step into the light

Step into the light, stream one final bow
Fear not the tiny tremors in my hands
Fairy spirit of green afterlife how
Once soft and poorly lied, now princely stands

Amongst blurred gods, their cries shall wing their way
While you, find your happy field, swaying wheat
Lost winds of meadow, sweeping grassy hay
Pale shells in wavy sands, all come to meet

Step into the light, as darkness dies now
Fresh folds cuddle in and all childhood flows
And we, who grip, our flimsy tears bestowed
Against the chill, the grief of bending woes

Soar above the roar, into the light, leave
Live again when living was better life
The earth does sigh and smile and suck to breathe
Crooked belly of the undergrowth grieves

Careless calls on the sunny bank of home
Chase on a freedom, of dune, of beach comb
Sad men see, your sore sun pulled to the west
Part body, for soul, as swift as air's guest

Incorruptible Dream

Somewhere between the cloud of imagination and one's running
stream of consciousness, lies the human's incorruptible dream.
The dream around which
one patterns and pins hopes.
Not hundreds of hopes but hundreds of thousands of hopes,
shielding the dream in defence of its purity,
in a single unbreakable chain.
An ambitious, complex dream, founded on love.
An untouchable love who feels; holding no monetary value;
a human's priceless possession.
An unquenchable love, thirsting with passions,
feeding on souls, yet not greedy.
Love, as the beauty of inexhaustible ends and infinite possibilities.

Place our dreamer on a dock, at the centre of a
curvaceous island bay:
he mulls, turning, tasting and chasing the dream
till all pleasures and parts grow the more glorious:
a dream so vivid it may even be real.
In reaching out his hands and stepping forward he may be moving
and breathing in its atmosphere now.

Yet the dream is not complete: for he waits patiently for one
woman.
The one who will transform his life from simple existence,
into the magical dream in which he has been truly living
an inexplicable contentment.
The twinkling lights across the water shine through
low-harbouring mists.
The last of a paddling, pink sun pushes out over sea,
setting alive the ripples and folds of waves, splintering into
shimmering fragments before being engulfed
by an oceanic bowl of iridescence.
It burns beyond the horizon, departing this world for
the next, bequeathing a smoky, charcoal-black sky.
In this realm the shooting stars flash their wishes,
clashing with planets, piercing the borders of monumental space.
To witness the power of nature's genius is to feel its
indestructible elements seeping into your soul
and driving you deeper into creativity.

The idealised dream gathers imperfections as it stretches
across time: perhaps in one breathless gasp
there is the sudden realisation it has gone.
It left long ago, severed at a point in the past
and in confusion melted into muddy waters:
disguised by gaiety or the blinded dreamer's trap.
Such mastered plans are seldom simple their conclusions
settled years back by an unfortunate shift in chance.
It is not so optimistically immune to disaster as once imagined.
How imbalanced is the world,
when it warns you not of other fated meetings?
Each consequence impacting on the other,
seconds in hours and hours in weeks.
How quickly these hopes mutate, their layers crumble away.
The inseparable years of building a dream
vanish into stardust.

Very soon his vulnerabilities lie open and raw.
Only the present; the time of living, breathing, touching,
comes to show him this:
how once his intensive eye held one captive
in its obsessive ownership of air.

He chose a woman.
She is unresponsive and cynical of his dream.
His dream, so tightly wrapped and bound,
now breaks and shatters into irretrievable puzzled fragments.

O dear girl – what a shot to kill him with the word of 'no'
or worse no word at all.
How you consumed him with a resounding silence,
deafening even the softest ear.
You, the closest to his heart;
by you, the greatest wound is cast.

II

LYRICS

Out Of Reach

Please, please look for me
My heart still believes
Please, please look for me
My heart still believes
Yet the more I wait, the more I will hide
And out of reach you go

Each time you are near
My words disappear
Each time you are near
My words disappear
Yet the more I think, the more I fear
And out of reach you go

Is this just a passing phase?
Come to take me everyday
Come to take me everyday

Leave, and we will live alone
Stay and we can be unknown
Stay and we can be unknown
Stop to see me standing there
And reach for me, reach for me

So, the days go drifting by
Sun, then moon have left the sky
Sun, then moon have left the sky

So, the days go drifting by
Sun, then moon have left the sky
Sun, then moon have left the sky

Soft with your words and silent am I
Reach for me, reach for me
Reach for me, reach for me

Please, please look for me
My heart still believes
Please, please look for me
My heart still believes
Yet the more I wait, the more I will hide
And out of reach you go, out of reach you go,
out of reach you go... *(fade)*

Where Have You Gone?

Where have you gone?
Have you left me for someone?
The memories will always live on and on

Where did you go?
How I miss you ever so
Remember sadness comes and there is woe

I came searching just to find you
Where have you gone?
I see no shadow here beside me
Where did you go?

These sunless days come fade again
What would have been!
And all our hope falls on sad ends

Will you think of coming home?
To find me tearful and alone
When will you come home?
Where are you?
Where have you gone?

Remember
I'll love you
Forever…

All Has Been Said

There's no hope here within
A heart heaves of sin
And so slowly
Oh so slowly
This love that's wearing thin

Here you stand in disguise
The secrets and the lies
Our times in sad demise
No promise made this time
All has been said

There's a sadness inside
A lost love, a lost pride
And I'm lonely
I'm so lonely
This pain for me to hide

Not a word in my head
Not a smile to be shed
Nothing is sung, nor read
Bitter tears fall instead
All has been said

You did choose
Now it's me you must lose
So you have fled
And love is dead.

Statue In The Rain

People came and people went
But no-one came for me
I waited till the skies turned grey
And all the world had gone away

I hoped you would be safe, while I was here
I hoped you would be safe, while I was here
Then we'd go safely from this place alone

But that was not to be
No-one came that day for me

chorus
(So) I became a statue in the rain
Now I know how it feels
To be left, to be lost, (to be) forgotten too
Like a statue in the rain
No-one came for me that day
Like a statue in the rain
No-one came for me that day

People went, they crossed my path
But no-one noticed me
I sheltered till the earth turned again
Still all the pain was slow to end

I hoped you would be safe, I wait in vain
I hoped you would be safe, I wait in vain
And we'll go safely from this place unknown

But that was not to be
No-one came that day for me…

chorus
(So) I became a statue in the rain
Now I know how it feels
To be left, to be lost, (to be) forgotten too
Like a statue in the rain
No-one came for me that day
Like a statue in the rain
No-one came for me that day

www.ingramcontent.com/pod-product-compliance
Ingram Content Group UK Ltd.
Pitfield, Milton Keynes, MK11 3LW, UK
UKHW020127250726
13967UKWH00002B/518

9 780957 498044